Letter From The Prison

J O Akinlabi

Letters From The Prison

Copyright © 2015

Published by New Generation Publishing in 2015

The author asserts the moral right under the Copyright, Designs and Patents Act 1988 to be identified as the author of this work.

All Rights reserved. No part of this publication may be reproduced, stored in a retrieval system or transmitted, in any form or by any means without the prior consent of the author, nor be otherwise circulated in any form of binding or cover other than that which it is published and without a similar condition being imposed on the subsequent purchaser.

Print Edition ISBN: 978-1-78507-463-9

The views in this book are those of the author and The Bible but they are general views only and readers are urged to consult the relevant and
qualified specialist for individual advice in particular situations.

www.newgeneration-publishing.com

Letter From The Prison

Contents

06	Every Individual Under The Microscope Deserve – Pity
08	Everybody on Earth wants Wealth, Health and Security
09	The False World
12	Power, Position, Money, toys and Sex are all Illusions
15	By our own Strength it is Impossible
18	Reality Curve
20	Working for Nothing
24	Spirituality
25	Fighting, Fighting, Fighting and Quarrelling
27	From Jesus' Teachings and Revelations we can conclude the Following
29	Globalisation
31	We are all in Hell
34	All their Teachings and Practices are Opposed to that of Christ and the Scriptures
35	Monthly Message from the Mother of God to Medjugorje and the world, 25 March 2003
36	Morning Prayer and Meditations
42	Our Father
45	The Need to Forgive
50	Reality and True Freedom
52	Learning Christ
54	Morning Prayer
55	Evening Prayer
57	The Advantages of Legionaries
59	Reality
59	The Bad News
62	The Good News
68	Message of our Lady from Medjugorje, 25 May 1988
69	Everyday Mental Activities of Three Categories of Men and Women
72	A Brief Meditation on the Rosary, Mysteries and Prayer
72	The Joyful Mysteries
74	Sorrowful Mysteries
77	Glorious Mysteries
79	The Mysteries of Light

Letter From The Prison

Author's Foreword

Dear Reader,

Due to the nature of my job, I have had the opportunity of going away, far from the madding crowd, with plenty of time for prayer, contemplation and recollection. I have met and lived with almost all nationalities. Encouraged by the messages of Our Lady of Medjugorje, and through the grace of God, I have read the Bible many times, and I am still reading it plus lots of commentaries and spiritual books by various authors, Jesuits among them. I pray the rosaries and the divine mercy every day and read the Imitation of Christ plus daily meditations for every day of the year, on the life of our Lord Jesus Christ, and try to live the Gospel.

As a legionary, I try to tell anybody I meet about Jesus and Mary, to help them to see that we are not Europeans, Africans, Americans, Asians; rich, or poor, and so on; but individual human beings created by God but lost due to sin. Using my wide knowledge of the world try to convince them of the insignificance of one person in a country and in the whole world, plus all the lies, illusions and miseries of life, ending up in death (Ecclus. Sir. 40:1-11).

Since no one individual human being on Earth can ever satisfy his or her sinful human nature that is, desire for money, food, sex and vainglory we all need Jesus, Mary and the Catholic Church to guide us in denying ourselves and making our way to Heaven, because only Jesus has the word of eternal life (John 6:68-69). He said: "Deny yourself, carry your cross every day and follow me."

Since everybody I have encountered has not been able to dispute me, I decided to put all the materials I use for evangelisation in this book and send it out, instead of hoarding the gift of God. We are all definitely *in prison on Earth*. How can a person who lived all his life in a village without electricity and pipe-borne water - especially in the third world (what sin has he or she committed?) - know about London or New York or Paris or the oceans?

So, nobody on Earth can know about Heaven without Jesus, Mary and the Catholic Church. See you in Heaven, where there are no rich or poor, or division or fighting; only friends of God.

By a converted seafarer

OBSERVATION: the gap between rich and poor is forever widening. If we poor (eighty percent of the world population) do not seek Heaven with all our hearts, minds and labour instead of waiting for miracles or fighting, we deserve pity because we shall loose out both ways, missing Heaven and not having a taste of the good things of the Earth. Both rich and poor are all working for God (Eph. 6:5-9). The majority of human beings are neither poor nor rich. In fact nobody is rich, only God is rich. Wealth is an illusion – (Psalm 49:1-20).

Letter From The Prison

Every Individual Under The Microscope Deserve – Pity

(1Cor. 15:19)

Any individual human being on Earth without Jesus deserves pity, because he/she is building all his/her life upon sand. Jesus said, "Anyone who hears these words of mine and does not obey them is Like a foolish man/woman who built his/her house on sand" (Matt. 7:26-27). That is, upon a false world of lies and illusion; an ever-changing, imperfect and unstable material world: human nature (Rom. 8:6-8), as proved beyond reasonable doubt by this book.

The Earth is a very big prison, with various big and small prisons - that is cities, towns and villages - all over the world, and we as individuals are living in our various tiny prisons within the prisons, labouring, fighting, quarrelling, daydreaming, worrying, suffering from boredom, tiredness, fear, anxiety, loneliness, all sorts of diseases and chasing the illusions that are money, toys and sex, with no peace of mind (Deut. 28:65-67) always waiting for something, finally getting tired at old age and dying - meaningless!

Thanks to God for sending Jesus to bring the good news to the poor, to proclaim liberty to those in prisons, to recover sight for the blind, freedom for the oppressed and announce that the time has come when the Lord will save his people (Luke 4:18-21).

We all blame others the Government, the Americans, and so on (Gen. 3:12-13) plus priests and the Church. Every individual is a hundred percent responsible for his or her own salvation (Luke 6:41-42).

Letter From The Prison

***Who is the Catholic Church? Jesus Christ,
The Eucharistic king of the universe.
Invisible (Heb. 11:1-3,6)***

All we talk about in the world are rich and poor, success and failure, good and bad, weak, strong and powerful, black, white, yellow, blue and green with all sorts of religion and ideas to suit, and fighting. We are always avoiding the main problem of every individual human being since the Fall after Creation: sins. Before God, we are all failures.

***JESUS (EUCHARIST) MARY (ROSARIES)
THE CATHOLIC CHURCH (THE NEW ARK)
ARE THE ANSWER BECAUSE NOBODY
CAN STOP ME FROM COMMITTING SIN
OR RAISE ME UP WHEN I DIE***

Letter From The Prison

Everybody on Earth wants Wealth, Health and Security

Why should God give to you and not me (or vice versa), when we are all the same - sinners - and there is only one God?
Who created everybody and everything? Who is America, Britain, China, Iraq, Coca-Cola, the. Government, NASA, and so on? *God is everything.* (Sirach 43:13-33).

The reality of life is sin, suffering, old age an incurable disease that leads to death.

A faith that denies reality is not a faith but a delusion, a fatal delusion due to self-centredness and sensuality: God did not give anybody anything; everything on Earth and in Heaven belongs to God.

Naked we come, naked we shall go. Seeking Heaven alone brings true happiness because everybody cannot be rich or poor. Life is a journey to Heaven.

JESUS (EUCHARIST) MARY (ROSARIES) THE CATHOLIC CHURCH (THE NEW ARK) ARE THE ANSWER

Idolatry is seeking happiness' on Earth, where there is nothing but lies, sorrows, illusions and death - foolish! (Ps 14:Rom. 1:21-31).

PRAY YOUR ROSARIES EVERY DAY

---

[1] *To be happy in this world of sins we must be using others. That is making somebody else unhappy, destroying the work of God. Sooner or latter we shall be used, since nobody gets away with evil.*

Letter From The Prison

The False World

How many people make decisions on behalf of millions?

As an individual, how much do we contribute to the major or minor decisions of our country and of the world? Most of us do not even vote.

How much do we know about our country - for example the origin of our fellow citizens and where we all come from? And where are those who lived there before us? *We are all unique individuals, power packed with all sorts of abilities and knowledge to be used for the glory of God but indoctrinated from birth.* Many do not know the name of their countries.

NOTE: Everybody in every country are not the same, so is every black people, white, Arabs, Indians, Chinese, and Jews and so on are not the same.

Government is a system that is using money, guns, bomb, intimidation and fear to bring different people together. No Love.

Those who make decisions, are they not adjusting to circumstances beyond their control? Only God is in control. *Because through confusion and struggles of ego against ego, God works toward its ultimate aim; nothing is lost, nothing is destroyed, in reality there is nothing but God.*

Those who invest all their life in their country without anything for the Kingdom of God - for example America, China, India, Nigeria; are America, China, India, Nigeria, and so on in Heaven? *In most cases these individuals are only seeking their own glory. They have no use for God.*

The doctors, policemen, politicians and lawyers who we all rely on for our health and justice, are they not weak human beings like you and me with individual personal problems like every other human being?

Those who claim to have lands and properties: how did they make the soil, trees, animals, water, air and the human beings who work for them?

Those of us with sons and daughters: how do we make their toes, their lovely noses, eyes, and what materials did we use for making the hair and where did we get them from and so on? Almost all of us do not listen to our parents. Infact Nobody Listen.

Where they give us the news about the whole world: that is about seven billion people and the life story of a sixty- year-old person - that is $60 \times 365 \times 24 = 525,600$ hours in under one hour and so on.

How can we prove that the child driving cows in the third world is not a whiz-kid or the girl in my village is not as beautiful as Miss World?

We shall never see the person called America or China and so on; only human beings, houses, cars, trees, animals, sun, moon, water and so on.

Since the world we live in is false, and we as individuals are lost in this massive world because of sin, Jesus came to save us and showed us the way back home. Hence he said, "I am the way, the truth and the life. Nobody comes to the Father except by me."

Jesus stands for peace, justice and reconciliation of the world

Anybody who is not for Jesus is against Jesus; that is against justice and peace in the world, because if we do not have peace in our heart, we cannot give it to others, and if Jesus is not dwelling in our heart we shall never have peace. He said:

Without Him we can do nothing;

Letter From The Prison

Because we are lost; He is the way;

We live in a false world; He is the truth;

We are dead in sin; He is life.

The Catholic Church is the answer. Beware of Religion which is the same as Politics, Nationalism, Patriotism, Tribalism and so on.

PRAY YOUR ROSARIES EVERY DAY

God has planned everything that is happening, that ever happened, that will happen long ago (Isa. 37: 26-28). Compared to the Domino principle, God has set everything and tipped it since Creation, and everything is falling into place accordingly. Only those who believe in Jesus Christ will see the end and the meaning of it all when we get to Heaven (Isa. 41:4; Judith 9:5-6). "Those who travelled on the highway called 'The Road of Holiness'" (Isa. 35:8-10).

JESUS (EUCHARIST) MARY (ROSARIES)
THE CATHOLIC CHURCH (THE NEW ARK)
ARE THE ANSWER

Power, Position, Money, Toys

Letter From The Prison

and Sex are all Illusions

Isa. 55:1-2

Power and Position

For every group, organisation, institution, and so on there must be a leader or a managing director, just as God is the general managing director of the Universe, a permanent position for ever. No one individual human being can occupy a position forever. Everything on Earth is a shadow of the invisible. People fear or obey the position, not the man or woman sitting on that chair; somebody else will be there tomorrow, and nobody on Earth has absolute power. In most cases they are adjusting to circumstances and compromising in order to hold on to power, but only God is in control, no human being.

Money and Toys

Technology started when God created man and let him loose to survive by himself, giving him knowledge and all the materials needed to survive. The early people needed fire; one way or the other they struck two stones and made fire. Ever since, people have been inventing things both as individuals and teams or by accident, adding to or subtracting from earlier inventions. For example, we cannot say Mr Jones "made" the Boeing 747 or Mr John "made" the internet. Necessity is the mother of invention.

As ordained by God, we should all work for our bread; money is to make the world go round. Nobody eats money. For example, if we have money we spend it; if we hoard it in the bank, the bank workers must survive; if we build a house, all the artisans involved and those making and selling the materials must survive; if we buy a car, people are busy in the car and steel industries making a living and our car does not drink water, we need fuel; the oil and shipping industries are there with human beings trying to earn a living, and so on. If we decide to choke ourselves with rubbish because of greed that is our problem, not God's. Whatever be our job, good or evil, God is using everything, and sooner or later we all be rewarded accordingly (Ecclus., Sir. 31:5-9).

Sex
Everybody on Earth loves sex, plus dogs and other animals. It is the cheapest thing on Earth and the problem of man and woman, some want it man and man, woman to woman, or just looking or talking about it, or by hand and so on. How can we prove that we enjoy it more than our neighbour? So many lies everywhere about sex prostitution, pornography and drugs. How nice to see a loved one, for example daughter or sister or brother a victim of this evil? Jesus said "Do unto others what you want others to do to you".

Power, money and sex are all illusions because everything in the Universe belongs to God; not our property. And we shall never have enough of these things, always wanting more, more, more. Without Jesus, prayer, and religious activities (Catholicism) to distract us, nobody is safe from all the temptations and evil everywhere around us, and we shall never know when to stop, until we are lost completely. That is why Jesus said, "What does it profit a man to gain the whole world and suffer the loss of his soul."

Natural religion or materialism and idolatry is a religion that does not need faith; that is, worshipping what man and God have made instead of worshiping God who is spirit the creator of everything and using them. (Wisdom 13:1).

JESUS (EUCHARIST) MARY (ROSARIES) THE CATHOLIC CHURCH (THE NEW ARK) ARE THE ANSWER

WE ARE ALL VICTIMS – For example, the black Africans have no History and scripts like the Chinese with the Great Wall; Indians with Taj Mahal; Egyptians with the Pyramids; the Greek Empire, Babylonians, Romans and so on. They are the Victims of the Arabs and the Europeans. Thanks to Jesus and Mary their only hope of Heaven.

They cannot make Nuclear Bombs, Submarines, Aircraft Carriers, Jet Planes, or drill crude oil, build Super Tankers and so on. All these are very good source of employment for Food, but they cannot save the World.

Most people in the bush are ignorant of all these things, but they all know about sin, death and Heaven.

ONLY JESUS CAN SAVE

Letter From The Prison

By our own Strength it is Impossible

God in Heaven (Rev. 7:9-17) REST IN PEACE

Peace of mind (Gal. 5:22-26) in the world but not of the world (John 17:15-16). Peace in the midst of the storm. Salvation is free (John 7:37-39).

We need Jesus (Eucharist), Mary (Rosary), and the Catholic church's teachings, practices and activities to fight the disordered and **insatiable desires** of our human nature every day. That is, life in the spirit and detachment from the world (Matt 5:20).

Baptism, being born again, conversion and continuous conversion of hearts, by refusing the Devil's lies and promises to be another God, and let God be God; that is, omnipotent, omniscience, omnipresent. And He lives forever.

Every individual shall give account of him/herself to God (Rom. 14:12).

God created all men and women in His own image (Gen. 1:27)

Africans, Americans, Chinese, Indians, Europeans, Jews, Arabs, and so on - in short all individual human beings on Earth - are on a journey from God back to God (2Macc. 7:22-29; Ezek. 18:4). From Dust to Dust we are all pilgrims as all our ancestors were (Psalm 39:12).

Letter From The Prison

To God belongs the Earth and all it contains, the world and all who live there.

↓

Everybody is born into sin, all gone astray (Isa. 53:6; Ps. 51:5; Rom. 11:32) all our hearts are anti-God. We all want our own ways; that is, to be another God, know everything (curiosity), be present everywhere (desire for travelling) and have unlimited power (greed) (Gen. 3:5) and we do not want to die.

↓

Self-imprisonment, self-centeredness, greed and sensuality (Ps. 36:1-4). Egoism.

↓

Gratification of the disordered and <u>insatiable desires</u> of our human nature by all means possible.

↓

All the evil in the world that you can think of (Gal. 5:19 - 21) plus natural or selfish religion/idolatry/anti-Christ; that is those gratifying their sinful nature under the mask of religion and virtue (Luke 11:37-52) or evil means.

↓

No peace of mind, always seeking rest where there is no rest (Deut. 28:65-67) and happiness where there is only sorrow. Money is not free anywhere in the world.

↓

Hell: since we are not God - there is only one God - we shall never fulfil our sinful nature, but adjusting to circumstances, end up in dust (Rom. 8:6). Hence so many lies (Rom. 3:4) everywhere to deceive others into Hell. Get out of Hell now before it is too late; after death it is impossible. A lot of people think that Hell is very sweet now just because of sensuality - childishness (1Cor. 13:11) and dissipation - foolishness (Ps. 53; Ps. 73: 17-20).

Eternal misery with the Devil (Rev. 21:8)

***JESUS (EUCHARIST) MARY (ROSARIES)
THE CATHOLIC CHURCH (THE NEW ARK)
ARE THE ANSWER***

Letter From The Prison

Reality Curve A Vicious Cycle

The individual life cycle of ungodly successful, not so successful and unsuccessful persons

The wicked in his arrogance does not look very far There is no God is his only thought (Ps. 10:4; Wisd. 2:1; 21-24).

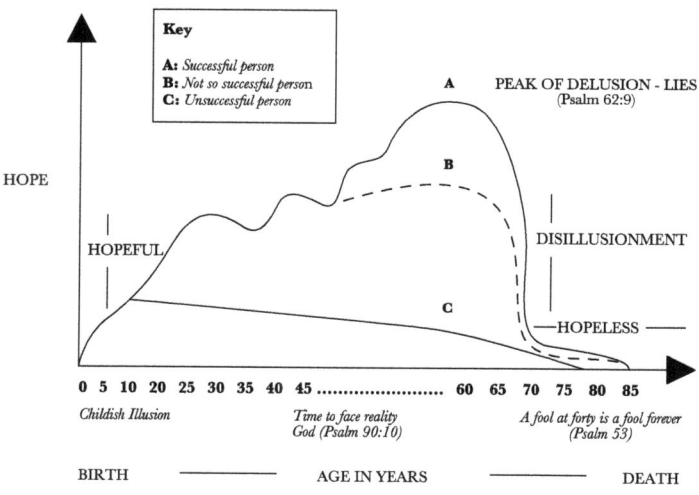

Pursuing futility they became futile (2Kgs. 17:14-18)

Meaningless, meaningless, everything is meaningless! What profit can we show for all our toil, toiling under the sun? A generation goes, a generation comes, yet the Earth stands firm for ever (Eccles. 1:2-11). Thanks to Jesus and Mary for bringing meaning into our life and history (John 8:51) and salvation is the only success there is, and it is given.

Letter From The Prison

READ THE GOSPEL AND PRAY YOUR ROSARIES EVERYDAY

The Bible did not just fall down from Heaven, it is the Catholic Church's property, and they are the best interpreters. If there is no Heaven the Bible is meaningless since all the characters in the Bible are dead except Jesus, and we are all going to die too. (John 8:51-53).

SERIOUS WARNING: Lying against God is called blasphemy an unforgivable sin against the Holy Spirit. Success is the source of pride; fame is the source of ruin.

No one has ever seen God. Christianity is faith from the beginning to the end, not feeling, hearing or seeing (Rom. 1:17-25). We all have no excuse for not having faith because the handwriting of God is on the wall everywhere (Acts 17:28). In God we live, move and exist. "'Blessed are those who believe without seeing,' says the Lord" (John 20:29).

NOTE: There is no America, Japan, Russia, Ghana, Guatemala, Sweden and so on in the Bible. Just the EARTH and is for nobody, only God.

Letter From The Prison

Working for Nothing

Under the yoke of the Devil (Matt. 11:28-30)

The main preoccupation of non-believers and non-practising Catholics, (they are the same) is money for pleasure and comfort; in short, to satisfy the senses - impossible! This is human nature. The eyes will never be tired of looking, and the ear will never be tired of hearing, and so on.

The Earth is God's vineyard; everybody on Earth knowingly or unknowingly is working for God, mainly to provide food for the table no matter the quality, to survive as a penance for original sin. Adam did it for nine hundred years.

Money is an incentive to encourage people to work, and a medium of exchange because no one person or country is self-sufficient, hence money must be spent for everybody on Earth to survive. That is to eat and go to the toilet.

Therefore non-believers and non-practising Catholics are working all their lives to feed others. Pity - only because they refused to believe in Jesus Christ and be saved they became a victim of the Devil, deceived through the senses, thinking all the while that they were working for themselves and enjoying it. Hence lying because nobody can satisfy the senses - illusion. For example, I have been all over the world, or to America *or* Europe, but I don't know everywhere in my village. NOTE: In my village, if you don't have money, nobody will reckon with you, so is everywhere in the world. No money no love. An American or a European does not know everywhere in his or her village, town or city. Even sex - everybody on Earth loves sex, but by the age of forty-five years we shall need loads of drugs. Foolish! to worship sex.

How can we get a reward from God if all along we have been

working for ourselves and our own glory? By the age of sixty years the race is practically over. Besides, no money is a hundred percent clean.

Jesus came to teach us about Heaven. No one has ever seen God and Heaven. Before Christ nobody knew about it, it was all speculation. Jesus taught us about Heaven with certainty and authority. It is a teaching completely opposed to our natural ways of thinking and living: supernatural - for example for a woman to have a baby without sexual intercourse or for a dead person to rise again after death. That is why up till today people are still anti-Christ and anti-Catholic.

NOTE: those in the world who do not believe in Jesus cannot receive the Holy Spirit, hence they can never see anything good about the Church or anything. They only stand far away throwing stones that cannot hurt a fly.

The Catholic Church is a school for learning about something completely new to our way of thinking and living for every individual. The success of every individual depends more on our own determination to go to Heaven, by doing our homework - that is prayer, studies - and putting into practice what we learn from the Church, and being prepared for the examination at any time. Death: only God, who sees the heart of every individual, will mark our papers and give the verdict, not the parish priest or Bishop who does not know every member of his congregation intimately or know what they are doing in their various homes and employments. *We shall never see a group, or congregation or a community that are all holy people. Some are spiritually advanced, some half way, some are backsliding, some are just starting and some are weeds.*

Since the beginning of the Church people have been trying to bring the Church to the level of our human, natural way of thinking. St Paul fought all his life to prevent the perversion, and all his letters serve that purpose. Christianity is life in the spirit of Christ, because "God is Spirit, and only by the power of His Spirit can people worship Him as He really is" (John 4:24; Phil. 3).

Most other churches or religious organisations are either patriotic or a religious model to suit the culture, human nature, feelings or emotions, whereas Christianity is practical; that is, learning to love everybody under any circumstances; we may find ourselves in union with Jesus (Eucharist).

NOTE: our feelings and emotions can be influenced by lots of things depending upon the surrounding environment, moods, ambition, alcohol, music, beautiful ladies for men and handsome men for women and so on.

All these can be compared to King Jeroboam who installed an idol in Israel to prevent the people from going over to Jerusalem, so that they would not transfer their allegiance to King Rehoboam of Judah (1Kgs. 12:26-27) which eventually led to their ruin.

During the early days of Christianity people thought the Roman Catholic Church was a Roman instrument for colonisation, even the third world thought Christianity was the European instrument for colonisation, hence there are so many types of Jesus on the market. People had to create the type of Jesus that suited their own kinds, culture, colours, classes, feelings, ambitions, emotions and so on, feeding their appetite according to St Paul, encouraging laziness (Rom. 16:17-18).

NOTE: voodoo worshipers in Haiti speak in tongues after working themselves up.

All these defeat the aim of God, trying with the Devil to destroy the plan of God. The aim of God is to reconcile to Himself all things, whether on Earth or in Heaven, making peace by the blood of His Cross (Col. 1:14-20; Col. 3:9-11).

In Heaven and in the grave there will be no Europeans, Africans, Americans Indians, Jews, Chinese, Arabs, Russians or class prejudice and division; only those who have washed their robes with the blood of the lamb from Europe, Africa, America, India; in short, from all walks of life; those who love Jesus, not using Jesus or trying to manipulate God (Rev. 7:9-17; Isa. 43:5-7).

Invariably unbelievers and non-practising Catholics are a medium of exchange too to pass money around, in order to feed the world since everything on Earth belongs to God.

JESUS (EUCHARIST) MARY (ROSARIES)
THE CATHOLIC CHURCH (THE NEW ARK)
ARE THE ANSWER

Letter From The Prison

Spirituality

There is no way to preserve our spirituality apart from silent suffering and labour, remaining faithful to the practice of solitude, and forgetfulness of all creatures and outward events, even though the world should disintegrate about us.

Never fail to keep your heart at peace and in tender love, ready to suffer as things present themselves.

It is impossible to make progress except by working and suffering courageously, always in silence.

To have God in everything a soul must have nothing in everything, for how can a heart belong in any way to two people at once?

When anything disagreeable happens to you, remember Christ was crucified and kept silent.

St John of the Cross

JESUS (EUCHARIST) MARY (ROSARIES)
THE CATHOLIC CHURCH (THE NEW ARK)
ARE THE ANSWER

Letter From The Prison

Fighting, Fighting, Fighting and Quarrelling

(James 4: 1-4)

This is all we have been doing since the Fall after Creation up till today; fighting. Fighting within ourselves - that is, no peace of mind - between families, between husband and wife, child and child, children and parents, with our neighbours, at home, at work, tribe against tribe, nation against nation; fighting everywhere under all sorts of disguises and schemes. Both civilised, uncivilised, educated, uneducated, rich, poor, Jews, gentiles; everybody is fighting one thing, one way or the other. It is fighting galore, no love and no peace because our soul is in prison and aching for freedom.

This is because everybody is born self-centred and naturally we all want to satisfy ourselves by all means possible. Wanting to be God, we all want money - the only means of satisfying our sinful human nature, that will give us pleasure, comfort, position, power, privileges and praises of people - to be God-like; this is called upward mobility, the spirit of the sinful world since we are not God - there is only one God who tolerates no rival - we shall never satisfy ourselves; hence fighting physically and/or interiorly in an attempt to satisfy ourselves, resulting in no peace of mind ("Restless will our heart be until it rest in you, O God," St Augustine).

Jesus Christ, Saviour of mankind who is God, came to give us a very simple message for every individual all over the world.

1) The Devil who caused this entire problem and made us enemies of God has been condemned (John 12:31; 16:11). His coming marks the beginning of the end of time (Heb. 1:1-4).

Letter From The Prison

2) He came to reconcile us with God and atoned for our sins (John 3:16) because it was not our fault, and the God we are all fighting loves us very much. "Nobody asked to be born a sinner or to come into this world of sins" (Rom. 5:8-11.)

3) Now stop fighting; forgive and love everybody. He taught us everything about God and how to stop fighting and we need him every day, minute and second to help us, that is the Eucharist - plus the rosary and other prayers. Downward mobility.

4) Now, since I have come to reconcile you with God, it is either you believe in me and stop fighting or continue fighting and perish with the Devil; who has been condemned - no more judgement. The choice is for every individual; for God or for the Devil (Mark. 16:16).

5) Now the only fight we need to fight is to fight ourselves to stop fighting; that is self-immolation by mortifications and interior struggles. Using his teachings, commandments, Eucharist, rosary, Divine Mercy, Stations of the Cross and other prayers as the weapon to start loving instead.

For any individual to wake up overnight and stop fighting is impossible because it is deeply rooted in us. So He founded His church (the Catholic Church) that has the road maps or sacraments and teachings which will help anybody \who wants to stop fighting and go to Heaven to stop because in Heaven there is no fighting only by practising the professed Catholic faith gradually, not just becoming a Catholic ; which leads nowhere but Hell.

Other organisations promise to teach us either how to manipulate God, or get round God or how to fight properly, or something somewhere that will help us win the fight that nobody has ever won - a losing battle - this is called idolatry. Since Jesus stands for peace, Anti- Christ stands for evil; that is, go on fighting, have it your own way, do not forgive, love only your own kind and cult, clubs, societies, fraternities, and so on.

WHY SHOULD SINNERS LIKE YOU AND ME BE ABLE TO SEE VISIONS, HEAR VOICES, PERFORM MIRACLES AND SPEAK TO GOD, AND YET OTHER SINNERS CANNOT?

JESUS (EUCHARIST) MARY (ROSARIES) THE CATHOLIC CHURCH (THE NEW ARK) ARE THE ANSWER

From Jesus' Teachings and Revelations we can Conclude the Following:

1) That we are not on Earth just to fight, fight; for sex, sex, money, money, toys, toys, food, food, drink, drink, and then to die like an animal without thinking. *Meaningless!*

2) That life is a burden, an adventure, a sacrifice, a challenge and a journey from God, seeking God from birth, growing slowly every day, in the knowledge of God, to maturity at old age until we see God face to face in Heaven after death, which will free us from bondage.

This makes life more meaningful and fulfils all our life. Through our faith in Jesus, we are always looking forward to God, our home with hope, loving God and our neighbours, and prayer will keep us busy all our life, in the midst of all the temptations, distractions, joys and sorrows that we experience daily (Matt. 6:34). Every day is a cross to bear.

Those who refuse to believe in Jesus have been judged already, they will get tired of chasing illusions with hard labour and get disillusioned at old age with nothing to look forward to and nothing to keep them busy before death; only boredom, loneliness, regret, worrying for nothing, still fighting, and quarrelling. Before the real death they are already dead in the head, see how the evildoer lie fallen battered and never to rise again (Psalm: 36:12). "Pursuing futility they became futile" (2Kgs. 17:15-16).

No matter how crafty we are we cannot reap where we did not sow or suddenly find God and Heaven which we had not been looking for after death. Repent before it is too late! Hence this present life is Hell to be confirmed by death for those who do not believe in Jesus and a trial period for believers (Rev. 7:13-17).

JESUS (EUCHARIST) MARY (ROSARIES)
THE CATHOLIC CHURCH (THE NEW ARK)
ARE THE ANSWER

Letter From The Prison

Globalisation

Globalisation is a reality only if Jesus Christ is the cornerstone. This plan, which God will complete when the time is right, is to bring all Creation together, everything in Heaven and on Earth, with Christ as head, (Eph: 1:10).

Imagine if the whole world were converted! That is, no more fighting. This is the main intention of Our Lady. Pray your rosaries every day for Her immaculate heart to triumph. If you are in doubt, be careful; you may miss out. During the siege of Samaria, there was a severe famine, so severe that mothers were eating their babies. The King consulted Elisha. He answered, "Listen to what the Lord says, by this time tomorrow you will be able to buy in Samaria three kilograms of the best wheat or six kilograms of barley for one piece of silver."

The personal attendant of the King said to Elisha, 'This can't happen, not even if the Lord Himself were to send grain at once."

"You will see it happen but you will never eat any of the food," Elisha replied. The prediction came true; the personal attendant saw it, but he was trampled to death at the gate by the people and died. He saw it happen but never ate any of the food (2Kgs. 6:24-7; 1-20).

Immaculate heart of Mary will triumph

"As for me and my families we shall be there" (1Cor. 15:51-54).

"Where there will be a banquet for all nations of the world" (Isa. 25:6-9).

"Nevertheless, the land will vomit the ungodly in God's own time" (Lev. 18:25-29).

Letter From The Prison

***JESUS (EUCHARIST) MARY (ROSARIES)
THE CATHOLIC CHURCH (THE NEW ARK)
ARE THE ANSWER***

PRAY YOUR ROSARIES EVERY DAY

Letter From The Prison

We are all in Hell

Only death will confirm it for those without Jesus Christ
To prove it: From what can be seen – Reality

1) Nobody is born holy except Mary; we are all born into sin.

2) Hence we are all self-centred, greedy and sensual; sex, sex, putting the whole world under the power of the evil one. We are not taught how to do evil, and we never listen, always bent on our own ways.

3) Evil is everywhere because we all want to satisfy ourselves by all means possible, some under the mask of virtues and religion.

4) Hence since Creation, as an individual and collectively, we have been fighting ourselves and our neighbours. No love, no peace, fighting for what is not our own. Since we can never obey all the commandments of God, we shall never have peace (Deut. 28:65-67), but hide under all sorts of consolations.

5) We shall never satisfy our selfishness and greed until we die. Neither will the true God satisfy any individual selfishness and greed because He has no favourites and is not a respecter of persons. He loves us all equally because He created us and maintains us in existence. He wants us all to be happy and safe. Nobody gets away with evil. We shall all suffer for our evil; hence so much suffering everywhere.

6) Three quarters of the world's population are jobless.

7) Three quarters of the earth's surface are uninhabitable - Ice, Deserts, Rocks, Mountains, Water, dangerous animals

and so on.

8) All sorts of natural and un-natural disasters - earthquakes, hurricanes, typhoon, flood, war, famine, fire, volcanic eruptions, epidemics and so on.

9) Majority of people on earth are restricted in their movements, not much travelling. Their only believe is the teachings of their ancestors – culture – and source of information are from their rulers – politics, from radio, TV, newspapers and rumours. (That is why a lot of religious people rely on visions and miracles).

10) We cannot see God now; neither can we see or hear ourselves; only the faults and miseries of others. After death we shall see God and ourselves.

11) Nobody is happy; only a few lucky ones? Happy because a lot of people are unhappy (the unhappiness of others is the happiness of a selfish person). Those who claim to be happy are living false lives, indulging in sensuality and dissipation; an illusory life; self-deception. Because God is the true source of happiness and everything they think is their own belongs to God, and He wants it for everybody.

12) So many lies everywhere in the name of this one God, using God as source of Income or for Politics and lying against God is called blasphemy – an unforgivable sin against the Holy Spirit.

13) Some people are ashamed to proclaim their faith in public; make jokes of God, serious matters and those who worship God; persecute holy objects and people but are not ashamed to do evil in public, boasting of what we should be ashamed of. Jesus said, "For those who declare publicly that they belong to me, I will do the same before my Father in Heaven. But if anyone rejects me publicly, I will reject him or her before my Father in Heaven" (Matt. 10:32-33). Sooner or later God will laugh at them when terror strikes (Prov. 1:26-29) and they will go into hiding.

14) Always on the lookout for bad news, daydreaming, gossiping and repeating the same stories.

Thanks to Jesus for establishing a safe haven on Earth - the Catholic Church - with a promise of a better life in Heaven!

If the Catholic Church is truly the church founded by God through Jesus, His only son - obviously it is (Matt. 16:18-19), since after two thousand years it is still waxing strong (Acts 5:38-39) - it stands to reason, then, that all other organisations are not from God; because since there is only one God, the same God and Jesus will never cause confusion by inspiring anybody to break up their body; they are for unity. Any inspiration from God should be to build up His Church. God is only bringing good out of evil, using them to model His Church to perfection. *All their teachings and practices are opposed to the teaching of Christ and the Scriptures; their faith is so strong that they deny reality and the words of God for selfish interest.* The best anybody can contribute to it is to graduate from the Church with flying colours - holiness - to be a Saint instead of causing troubles and division.

If we are not looking for God and Heaven, how can we suddenly find God after death? Just as we cannot go to the bank and cash money if we haven't got money there.

OUT OF SIGHT IS OUT OF MIND AND
THE SHOW MUST GO ON

JESUS (EUCHARIST) MARY (ROSARIES)
THE CATHOLIC CHURCH (THE NEW ARK)
ARE THE ANSWER

Letter From The Prison

All their Teachings and Practices are Opposed to that of Christ and the Scriptures

Their faith is so strong that they denied reality and the words of God for their selfish ends

We are all born free to worship God or not to. Every Religion and Secular clubs, fraternities, societies and so on, has its own believes, doctrines, rules and regulations and modes of worship.

To be a Christian is to follow Jesus Christ with his teachings and commandments. Anybody who changes his teachings sayings and commandments is an anti-christ. (Philippians 3:17-4:1)

JESUS (EUCHARIST) MARY (ROSARIES) THE CATHOLIC CHURCH (THE NEW ARK) ARE THE ANSWER

Letter From The Prison

Monthly message from the Mother of God to Medjugorje and the world, 25 March 2003

"Dear children,

"Also today I call you to pray for peace. Pray with the heart, little children, and do not lose hope because God loves His creatures. He desires to save you, one by one, through my coming here.

"I call you to the way of holiness. Pray, and in prayer you are open to God's will; in this way, in everything you do, you realise God's plan in you and through you.

"Thank you for having responded to my call."

JESUS (EUCHARIST) MARY (ROSARIES)
THE CATHOLIC CHURCH (THE NEW ARK)
ARE THE ANSWER

Letter From The Prison

Morning Prayer and Meditations

I believe in one omnipotent, omnipresent, omniscient God, the creator of Heaven, Earth and all things visible and invisible, the owner of everything.

1) I did not create myself I did not ask to come into this world of sin and suffering. I never knew when I fell asleep; now I am awake again today; I want to love you, unsleeping Lord. Every day is new and completely different from other days. Where am I coming from, what am I doing here and where am I going? Yesterday is gone, tomorrow is uncertain; only today is in my possession to seek God, the challenge and adventure we are made for (Eccles. 12:13-14).

2) There are billions of other beings like me out there in Asia, America, Africa, Europe, Oceania – Lost.

Some are just waking up like me; to another day of problems. If there is no problem that is another problem – Boredom.

Some are just going to bed after night duty or in another part of the World.

Some are in warm climate, a very hot climate sweating, or a very cold climate freezing, all striving to survive after survival we want to be rich.

Some have been working all night in industries, hospitals and hotels.

Some are working in the Lord's vineyard for the salvation of souls and of the world; that is the Pope, Cardinals, Bishops, priests, Seminarians, nuns, monks, brothers, Reverence Sisters and religious people and so on. A permanent job for Life and Eternity.

Letter From The Prison

Some are running the secular world; that is Presidents, Vice-Presidents, Governors, Ministers, Secretaries of state, Commissioners, Chief Justices, Vice Chancellors Chief Executives, Counsellors, Military Chiefs and so on. A temporary job for a certain period – political.

Some are suffering persecution for proclaiming Jesus. May the Lord and Our Lady strengthen them in their suffering. Amen.

Some are on their way to work, some are in hospitals, mental homes, leprosy camps and prisons. Some have been restless due to illness, worrying, fear and anxiety or nursing a sick baby or disabled person or rolling and pitching at sea.

Some are now too tired in old age, waiting for death to release them from bondage.

Some are on the war front or fighting and quarrelling at home or at work.

Some are in the air, at sea, on the train, in the mine, on military duties; for example policemen, customs officers, ambulance workers, immigration officers, prison wardens, soldiers, coastguards, Air Force Officers, Naval Officers, and so on as a means of earning their daily bread.

Some have been doing evil all night, robbery, pornography, smuggling, prostitution. What is their future?

Some earning their living in the red light districts.

Some children are on the street, homeless without parents as young as four years old.

Some are living a dissipated, idle and sensual life, that is gossiping, drunkenness and drugs, excessive pleasure, which is the flipside of despair and so on.

Letter From The Prison

Some are on the street, homeless and drugs victims.

Some are refugee's victims of war and violence.

Some are starving to death while food is being wasted somewhere.

Some are living in densely populated areas and countries.

Some are in the cities, towns and villages with no electricity.

Some are going from village, to town to city and vice versa.

Some are at home, bored, lonely and jobless, smoking themselves up.

Some are illegal immigrants looking for greener pasture.

Some are shining and smiling on the outside but running aching and crying on the inside.

Some are roaming about aimlessly.

Some are just starting family life while some are breaking up. Some are just coming into the world and some just going away; that is dying; about one or two million die every day. I may be one of that number today. Into Your hands, O God, I commit my spirit.

Some are in the mortuary (Sirach 41:1-14)

Plus millions of various activities going on in all the big and small airports and sea ports, train stations, Panama Canal, Suez Canal, Kiel Canal, Great Lakes, NASA, rivers, aircraft and ship-building industries, dry-docking and repair yards, iron and steel industries, military equipments, chemical field, oil exploration and production field, dams roads, bridges, skyscrapers, locks and docks, construction firms, the world of sports, farming, education, banking, insurance, Hotels, communications, Super Markets, entertainment, book publication, the blind and silent world, and so on; the list is endless. Millions will die in their tiny little prison with their own false, little happiness and religion complacent, thinking all the while that they are something we are only what we think we are, whereas we are nothing without God (Gal. 6:3). Self-centeredness is a chronic, subtle and deadly disease. "We have eyes to see and ears to hear so that we can be converted" (Acts 28:25-27).

And billions of other created things are out there: fish, birds, animals, insects, trees, the sun, moon, stars, milky way, galaxies and so on. To know this Mighty God is impossible for me; I need Jesus, who reveals to us the truth about God. He said, "The obstacle between us and God is sin, and if we believe in Him our sins will be forgiven and with His help and following His examples, teachings and commandments, we shall start learning how to love and if we persevere we shall be happy with God for ever in Heaven - eternal life after death. Without this life has no meaning."

First of all, I must confess that I am as sinful as the worse sinner out there (Titus 3:3).

Christ Jesus came into the world to save sinners, I am the worst of them, but God was merciful to me in order that Christ Jesus might show his full patience in dealing with me, the worst of sinners, as an example for all those who would later believe in Him and receive eternal life. To the eternal King, immortal and invisible, the only God, to Him be honour and glory forever and ever! Amen (1Tim. 1:15-17).

Father, please forgive my sins and help me to avoid every occasion of sin today.

Jesus, without you in my heart and my mind, I am going to be in trouble today; because millions of thoughts have rushed into my head on my waking up (for example, pride; that is, an inordinate, love of our own glory, ambition, rebellion, hatred, vengeance, injustice, seeking consolation in talking, news, TV, sex or masturbation where there is no consolation due to boredom and loneliness). That is why you said the way to Hell is very wide; out of the millions of thoughts rushing, into my head only your way, the way of self-denial and renunciation is the way to life, not my own ways; that is why you said, 'I am the way, the truth and the life; no one comes to the Father except by me."

Therefore, Father, give me the Holy Spirit, which is the gift from you to those who believe in Jesus and His Church. Without the Holy Spirit we cannot live a good Christian life; again that is why, Jesus, you said, 'Without me you can do nothing."

I invite Jesus again this morning to be born into my heart and the Holy Spirit to kindle in my heart the love of God.

Thank you, Mother Mary, the mediatrix of all grace, for all the graces bestowed upon me.

Without Jesus, Mary, the Catholic Church and learning from the Saints, who will ever know the way to God? Using all my knowledge, feelings and circumstances alone I am going to make up an idol (a God as small as myself, a poor, wretched God), be a fanatic; that is, over-exaggerate God or oversimplify God, that is, taking the mercy of God for granted, or be enslaved by somebody, people or things. No one individual will be able to know everything in the Bible and about the Church; thousands of people have contributed to the Church since Jesus and the Apostles, Saints, Fathers and Doctors of the Church. What is my own contribution? Building up or destroying?

Following your command, Jesus, you said, "Do not worry about tomorrow, it will have enough worries of its own. There is no need to add to the troubles of today, watch and pray always." Hence the battle of every day is to do the will of God under any circumstances we may find ourselves, which require mortifications and interior struggles.

Letter From The Prison

Please God, help me today. Everyone's Life is a Book – one page a day.

***JESUS (EUCHARIST) MARY (ROSARIES)
THE CATHOLIC CHURCH (THE NEW ARK)
ARE THE ANSWER***

Letter From The Prison

Our Father

The only Prayer Jesus taught us (Christianity is practical)

PRAYER: **MEDIATIONS:**

To call God our Father
The father of white, black, yellow, blue, green, rich, poor; in short, the Father of all human race, all tribes and nations.

Who art in Heaven
Not in London, New York, Mumbai, Paris, Moscow, Lagos, big names; not anywhere on Earth but in Heaven and everywhere in reality. We are all looking for God but in the wrong places. Let us look into our hearts. "He is with us always, knocking at the door of our hearts" (Rev. 3:20).

Hallowed be Thy name (the fear of God is the beginning of wisdom)
In the pubs, on the television, everywhere, they make jokes about God and those who worship God, and there are foul language and dirty jokes everywhere. Those who have no use for God will soon go and hide because of shame (Ps. 1:1).

Thy Kingdom come
Where there will be justice and peace, no drugs, pornography, division, bribery, corruption, war, fighting, quarrelling, gossiping, daydreaming, but love.

Letter From The Prison

Thy will be done on Earth as it is in Heaven

The sun, moon, stars, and so on; that is, all Heavenly beings and nature obey God, only we human beings want in our own ways to be another God. We should try, with the minimum of effort possible, to start giving in to God, for our own good, because we shall never win God, only destroy ourselves, body and soul. Jesus said, "Do not be afraid of those who kill the body but cannot kill the soul; rather be afraid of God, who can destroy both body and soul in Hell" (Luke 12:4-6). Whether we like it or not the will of God will be done today. Not even a sparrow drops dead without the knowledge of God.

Give us this day our daily bread. (No idle mind; if we are not seeking God with all our hearts and minds, (Deut. 6:4-9) the Devil is standing by twenty-four hours to tempt us. The Devil has gotten everybody already, because nobody is born holy, we have to fight to get out of his grip.)

Trust in God, He created us and He loved us, and maintains us in existence. Everybody on Earth can testify to a miracle and the goodness of God in their lives, both believers and nonbelievers. We are all ungrateful, biting the finger that is feeding us (Luke 6:35). Just face the problems of today squarely. If there is no physical labour, pray the rosaries or study the Bible or good books to learn about God and His Creation instead of worrying about tomorrow or wasting the precious today. Try to pray always, we pray with our hearts not with our hands, for example, Jesus, help me to love you. Whatever we are doing, if the aim is not for the glory of God, it is a waste with adverse effect.

Letter From The Prison

Forgive us our trespasses as we forgive those who trespass against us

This is the main core of Christianity - reconciliation of the world with God. For our sins to be forgiven we must forgive others. No more judgement; we shall judge ourselves. Forgiveness is every minute and every second's job, it is mainly from the heart, and without it we shall never have peace. Keep on trying to forgive; it is worth the effort.

Lead us not into temptation, but deliver us from evil. (Self denial and mortification are the answer. We shall never satisfy ourselves, but get into trouble, and God and people will laugh at our distress.) (Prov: 1:26-29).

We are all very weak. Avoid every occasion of sin; we should not trust ourselves, but spend more time with Jesus in the blessed sacrament and receive Him (Eucharist) often for spiritual strength. The Devil is very powerful.

JESUS (EUCHARIST) MARY (ROSARIES)
THE CATHOLIC CHURCH (THE NEW ARK)
ARE THE ANSWER

Letter From The Prison

The Need to Forgive

We are sinners and we Live among Sinners

1) First and foremost, if we have been living our life according to the will of God - that is, living a holy life – we shall have no cause to bear grudges with anybody, so in most cases we are the guilty one. *Forgive.*

2) We must have hurt someone, somewhere, sometime in the past; if not we have every right to cast the first stone. *Forgive.*

3) All our decisions at any given time are influenced by many things, ranging from our own conscious and unconscious motives, desires, moods, the pressure around us - called heat of the moment and surrounding atmosphere; for example, fearful, comfortable and so on. It is only afterwards that we shall start finding excuses to defend or deny them. Despite the fact that we think we are always in control; nobody is in control. *Forgive.* That is why Christians are advised to avoid occasions of sin; for example, unnecessary visits, idleness, meddling in other peoples' affairs.

4) No matter how careful we are, we still forget things and make mistakes. *Forgive.* It will get worse with old age.

5) We shall be hurting within ourselves any time we remember or see the party involved, while he or she is having a nice time. *Forgive.*

6) Everything on Earth belongs to God, nothing is our property; we haven't lost anything that is ours. *Forgive.* Naked we come, naked we shall go.

7) Human nature seeking the easy way out, that is, comfort, pleasure, false freedom, security in material things and so on; when we can't get these things we blame someone or something. A fatal delusion, there is no easy way to life; it is a burden, a challenge and a sacrifice to every human being born on Earth. We are all deceiving ourselves by hiding under endless news, talking, entertainment, hobbies, pleasures and so on. *Forgive.*

8) Since everything about every individual is inherited from both parents and circumstances from the womb to adulthood, if we have to blame anybody, we should blame God, who is responsible for creating all things visible and invisible. That was why He came down taking up all the punishments on Himself to atone for our sins. This same God is more or less begging us by saying to us:

- Forgive and keep on forgiving under any circumstances, because whatever is done to you is done to me.

- Tolerate everybody because all of you are my children.

- Trust and believe in me, I created all of you for myself; I am doing everything for your own good, though you may not see it now.

- I love you, you are very, very precious to me, more than sparrows. Don't be worried and anxious about anything - look at the birds in the sky, they do not sow or reap, they gather nothing into the barn, yet I feed them.

- Do not be afraid of those who can only kill the body. Where are those who killed Jesus and the Martyrs? Sooner or later we are all going to die anyway, a hundred years from now everybody alive now will all be dead; seven billion beings.

- Your name is written on the palm of My hand and I know the number of your hairs.

Letter From The Prison

- "I have redeemed you and call you by your name you are mine" (Isa. 43:1-2).

- Just be patient and persevere; keep on trying, it is only for a little while. I am with you always till the end of time. "Those that wait upon the Lord, will regain their strength; they will sprout wings like eagles, though they run, they will not grow weary, though they walk, they will never tire" (Isa. 40:31).

- Be still and know that I am God. Stop fretting.

- For my thoughts are not your thoughts and your ways are not my ways; my ways are above yours as the Heavens are as high above the Earth, my thoughts above your thoughts. For as the rain and snow come down from the sky and do not return before having watered the Earth, fertilising it and making it germinate to provide seeds for the sewer and food to eat; so it is with the word that goes from my mouth; it will not return to me unfulfilled or before having carried out and having achieved what it was sent to do (Isa. 55:8-11).

- Can a woman forget her baby at the breast; feel no pity for the child she has borne? Even if these were to forget, I shall not forget you (Isa. 49:15). "Vengeance is mine,' says the Lord. 'I myself shall fight those who fight you'" and:

- "I myself shall save your children, I shall make your oppressors eat their own flesh" (Isa. 49:25-26).

- Pray for your enemies, they deserve more pity than anger. That was why I asked my father to forgive us because we don't know what we are doing.

- Remember all things work together unto good for those who love God and through confusion and struggle of ego against ego, God works towards his ultimate purpose.

Letter From The Prison

- God brings good out of evil (Gen. 50:18-20).

- On your part do not commit sins for any reason on Earth, stand by, praying and watch.

- The Lord will do the fighting for you, you have only to keep still (Ex 14:4).

- Besides some of our enemies are more powerful than us and there is nothing we can do to them. *Forgive.*

- If the person you find it hard to forgive should ask God for forgiveness he/she will be forgiven.

- What God is doing to us through others, sickness and circumstances surrounding us, are.

1) To break our reliance on and attachment to the world, creatures, money and material things.

2) To get our attention; that is, free us from our self imprisonment and humble us.

3) To seal our tongues because we make to much noise; see Psalm 19:1-4.

4) To lure us into the desert and seduce our heart (Hos. 2:16) bringing us to an insolating experience, solely for Himself alone; He is a jealous God.

5) Thereby bringing us to eternal life, which He created us for: Heaven! He will continue to pursue us till the last day of our life on Earth. If we ever find ourselves in Hell, it is not His fault because we refused to listen and see (Isa. 6:9-10).

After all is said and done to forgive from the bottom of our hearts is hard, but forgive we must, because it is the basis of our own forgiveness and eternal salvation. Forgive us our sins as we forgive those who sin against us. This is why the rosary is a good weapon.

PRAY YOUR ROSARIES EVERY DAY

***JESUS (EUCHARIST) MARY (ROSARIES)
THE CATHOLIC CHURCH (THE NEW ARK)
ARE THE ANSWER***

Letter From The Prison

Reality and True Freedom

The heart, mind and reason of every individual human being born on Earth (about six billion) is trapped, restricted, modelled, enslaved by sin and circumstances - for example culture; superstitions, desire for temporal influence and prestige; vanity, money and sensuality, surrounding us from birth. Therefore relying on our own strength of mind and reason alone, we shall never be free and ascend to God in Heaven, our home.

Only by learning about Christ can anybody know the truth and be set free. That is why He said, "I am the way; the truth and the life; no one goes to the father except by me" (John 14:6). It is He who reveals to us the truth about God; because nobody has ever seen God (John 11:8).

A brief summary: the problem of every individual is in his/her heart (Matt. 15:15-20; Eccles. 9:3; Jer. 17:9-11) because before we do anything it is always premeditated

We are on the conveyor belt of a big production plant being carried away whether we like it or not; that is, from birth growing daily to old age and to death – then Heaven or Hell. The life of man/woman is not in his/her own hands (Jer. 10:23). Life of man/woman is like flower blooming in the morning and withering in the evening or like a shadow or a smoke. (Psalm 90:1-17). (Psalm 39:1-13).

Without Jesus life has no meaning. This is the history of man for the past six thousand years until the end of time. Without Jesus, Mary, the Catholic Church and the Saints, nobody can know the way to Heaven. The only way we know is the way to Hell.

Letter From The Prison

***JESUS (EUCHARIST) MARY (ROSARIES)
THE CATHOLIC CHURCH (THE NEW ARK)
ARE THE ANSWER***

Letter From The Prison

Learning Christ

In all the events of life, Teach me, my Lord, to be sweet and gentle

In disappointments,

In the thoughtlessness of others

In the insecurity of those I trusted,

In the unfaithfulness of those on whom I relied,

Let me put myself aside,

To think of the happiness of others,

To hide my little pains and heartaches,

So that I may be the only one to suffer from them.

Teach me to profit by the suffering that comes across my path.

Let me so use it that it may mellow me, not harden nor embitter me;

That it may make me patient, not irritable,

That it may make me broad in my forgiveness;

Not narrow, haughty and overbearing.

May no one be less good for having come within my influence, no one less pure, less true, less kind, less notable for having been a fellow-traveller in our journey toward eternal life.

As I go my rounds from one distraction to another, let me whisper

Letter From The Prison

from time to time, a word of love to Thee. May my life be lived in the supernatural, full of power for good, and strong in its purpose of sanctity. Amen.

Morning Prayer

O God, Lord of all good life, help me to use today well.

Help me to use today:

To know You a little better,

To do my work a little more diligently;

To serve my fellow men a little more lovingly;

To make myself, by Your help, a little more like Jesus.

Help me make today a day of progress in my life, and to become a little more like what You want me to be.

This I ask for Jesus' sake. Amen.

Letter From The Prison

Evening Prayer

Forgive me, O Father, for anything I refused to do today, which I might have done.

Forgive me for any help I might have given today, and did not give. Forgive me for being so wrapped up in my own troubles and my own problems that I had no time for those of anyone else.

Forgive me for being so immersed in my own leisure and comfort, and for refusing to give them up to help others, or to help Your Church and Your people and your work.

Help me to learn the lesson - I know that it is true - that selfishness and happiness can never go together; and help me to find happiness in trying to forget myself and in trying to bring help and happiness to others; through Jesus Christ my Lord. Amen.

William Barclay
More Prayers for the Common Man
(Harper Collins)

Letter From The Prison

The Full Meaning of Joy

JESUS FIRST

OTHERS NEXT

YOURSELF LAST

JESUS (EUCHARIST) MARY (ROSARIES)
THE CATHOLIC CHURCH (THE NEW ARK)
ARE THE ANSWER

Where two or three or more are gathered together without Jesus doing good and useful work; Don't worry they are talking

rubbish – gossiping or consoling themselves or

repeating the same stories or planning evil.

Letter From The Prison

The Advantages of Legionaries

After making that decision to follow Jesus, because it is the love of Jesus that urges us on, it will help us to get out of our self-imprisonment - the bad news.

1) By mixing with other people who are not our own kinds, colour and classes for Christ's sake.

2) Filled with the Holy Spirit we overcome our laziness and false self-shame, become bold, by obeying Jesus' command to go and tell others about Him - the good news.

3) We learn to take insults like Jesus, and "no" for an answer and become humble.

4) We have to smile at everybody, because we want to tell them about Jesus, thereby breaking down the barrier of division.

5) We study more, to be able to break down all self- defences because deep down everybody knows the truth, only hiding or hoping to get away scot-free.

6) We start learning to cure ourselves instead of curing others and the world, by practising what we preach.

Note: Everybody knows how to preach; b) Everybody in the world is the problem of the world

7) We become humble, firm and tough by rising after every fall. We are going to fall a lot because we don't listen and the road is rough and long, but it is one second compared with eternity.

8) We start learning to pray, because prayer is the narrow road nobody likes.

Always remember Mother Theresa, she said, "God has not called me to be successful, but to be faithful."

And St Therese of Lisieux: "Discouragement is another form of pride."

And St Thomas Aquinas said: 'When confronting an unbeliever or other sects, do not quote the Bible, use reason."

OUR LADY OF PERPETUAL HELP! PRAY FOR US

JESUS (EUCHARIST) MARY (ROSARIES)
THE CATHOLIC CHURCH (THE NEW ARK)
ARE THE ANSWER

Letter From The Prison

Reality

If there is no bad news, no good news

The Bad News

Everybody on Earth wants to be happy, encouraged by all the lies and temptations from the world around us and the Devil, always promising us that we can be happy if we can do this or that from childhood until we enter the grave, always hoping and doing everything within our power to be successful in order to be happy. To be happy in this world of sins we need money. God will never give a sinner money to be happy in sin, because to sin is to destroy ourselves, our neighbours and the work of God (1John 2:15-17). Hence:

1) We have to get that money one way or the other, with a lot of labour, worrying, fear, anxiety and so on, sometimes fighting and quarrelling, and to the extent of worshiping idols. We shall never get enough money for that happiness. Illusions!

2) We shall loose all the money one way or the other because we must spend it and everything on Earth belongs to God; not our property - naked we come naked we shall go.

3) Somebody or other must get hurt if we want to be happy by all means.

4) When we cannot get it we start fighting.

5) All the happiness of the world is only on the outside; laughing and smiling with plenty of problems inside, no peace of mind only hiding under all sorts of consolations, blaming and confessing the sins of others because it is always them not me.

6) Coupled with the facts that every human being on Earth has all the natural problem, for example, sicknesses, because nobody is well, and it gets worse with age, worrying, boredom, loneliness, one problem or the other with our neighbours, tiredness, fear of the future and of death, old age, always waiting for something and eventually death. What a happiness! No sinner is happy in this world it is all lies, lies, and lies (Deut. 28:65-67).

Letter From The Prison

What is True Happiness?

Obeying the Laws of God, written in our hearts, because we all know what is good and bad, and doing His will.

Unfortunately nobody has obeyed all the laws of God ever since God gave the laws to Moses, hence up till today religion has become a very controversial and sensitive issues, because some bodies or groups of people are always imposing the laws of God and Jesus or their own ideas on others, while they themselves cannot obey them, and they have plenty of natural problems like every one of us.

Hence the new covenant; the law of the Spirit, because God is Spirit. Only by the power of the Spirit can we worship God (Phil.3:8-ll). It is only God that can see the heart of every human being on Earth, and knows what every individual is doing from conception to death (Psalm 139:1-24).

Letter From The Prison

The Good News

Salvation - that is, Jesus the man-God coming to save us from destroying ourselves, our neighbour and the world we live in. We don't become Christians overnight, we have to do our homework to find out the following:

1) Who is Jesus? How can a human being claim to be God? Because nobody has ever seen God, is He really God? All these involve thoroughly investigating Jewish history and culture - the origin of the man-God and why they were expecting a messiah - in order to understand the Gospel stories.

2) Other religions and other types of Jesus on the market. What do they promise us, and what does the real Catholic Jesus promise us? We should compare both with realities, and then make up your minds which of the God or Gods we want to worship. Is it Baal or the true and only one God, which Jesus has made known. It would be a fatal mistake to assume that all religions are the same, worshiping the same God; there is only one God, one faith, one hope and one Lord. Everybody in the world believes in God, due to circumstances and cultures, every nation, tribes and talented individuals have made up their own mistaken ideas of what the true God is. Jesus came to make the true God known (John 17:3). In other words, to reconcile the world with God.

As for me, after thorough studies, investigations and my journey to many places all over the world (I was not a Catholic, and I have read the Bible more than ten times plus other books and the history of Christianity and other religions), the Catholic Jesus present in the Eucharist and in the blessed sacrament of the altar is the true God I want to worship and serve. He is the true Bread of Life,

Letter From The Prison

readily available everywhere all over the world, and not restricted to Rome or a Basilica or a Cathedral or any one place alone.

For example, I have attended masses in many churches all over the world, neither the Priest nor anybody in the congregation knew who I was or my heart, and vice versa. Note: All the countries that I have visited, the rulers of these countries will never know that I was in their country and everybody I meet in the streets and city centres do not know who I am and vice versa. Only God knows everything. Vain glory is an evil plague.

It is my faith in Jesus present in the Eucharist and His Church that is leading me on. *For me, this proves Jesus' statement: "No one comes to the Father except by me" beyond reasonable doubt. Because only God sees the heart of all human beings and since all our hearts are evil because we are sinners, the way to see God is only with Jesus, our Saviour and advocate in our hearts and on our lips at the point of death.*

1) The first condition for salvation is to believe that Jesus is the true God and true man. Observe all the miracles of healing in the Gospel. He always asked them, "Do you believe in me?" As for me, I believe with all my heart.

2) When we profess our faith in Him, He will ask *them* and us, "What do you want me to do for you?" As for me I was baptised a Catholic when I was thirty-nine years old in Liverpool. I had lived all those years in sin looking for happiness, like every other human being; one of the problems of the world, (everybody in the world is the problem of the world) so I was very sick, almost dead spiritually. I implored Him to have mercy on me, a miserable sinner, that I wanted to see and be well again. He said, "Go and sin no more." Then He said my faith had made me well and to go and sin no more and start putting into practice all my teachings and commandments or else something worse would happen to me (Luke 6:46-49).

Letter From The Prison

The greatest problem for all believers in Jesus after that first encounter or conversion is following Him along the narrow road, putting into practice His teachings and commandments until death, which is very hard. Hence a lot of Christians and religious organisations have decided to make the road wider to suit themselves. That is, miracles, or rice or water down Christianity. What a delusion!

Only the Catholic Church - the biggest bank of spiritual treasures on Earth, that is still preserving the teachings of Christ unpolluted after two thousand years, that can accommodate all the sinners in the world who want to go to Heaven, with the help and assistance from Saints, those who had gone ahead of us following in the footsteps of the master, coupled with the greatest of all intercessors, Mary, mediatrix of all graces, the mother of the man-God - offers the best platform for practising the teachings and commandments of Christ gradually, because nobody on Earth can stop committing sins overnight. The sacrament of reconciliation helps us to start again when we fall. By putting our faith into practice little by little, that is when we shall get all the graces we need to continue.

To follow Jesus is a journey of faith all our life for every individual (Luke 14:26-27) because we have no control or power over the hearts of others and vice versa. According to masters of spiritual life, we shall never attain the perfection Christ is demanding from us here on Earth; all that is demanded of us is a genuine effort to keep on trying till the end of our lives on Earth.

We shall only succeed in deceiving ourselves, encouraged by those who patronize us, because we cannot see ourselves or deceive others and God, if we are not conversant with our Bible, especially the Gospel with the New Testament, where we shall get to know Jesus more and more every day and learn his teachings and commandments in order to put them into practice.

I attended a requiem mass once. After the Priest had performed all the necessary requirements, he placed the Bible on top of the coffin and said he/she had been living his/her life according to the Gospel; very frightening because most Catholics don't read their Bible. How on Earth can they know about Jesus and His teachings, except making up their own wide road back to Hell?

The true Catholic, Jesus, did not promise anybody happiness in this world of sins only self-denial and sacrifice for our neighbours and for God which require suffering, with a promise of a better life after death - eternal life.

The alternative is to suffer for nothing, because to be happy in sin involves more suffering and we shall end up choking ourselves to death for the rich or starving to death for the poor because we shall never satisfy ourselves.

Only Jesus has the best idea of saving the world. He said:

(1) For the rich: if you want to come with me to Heaven, no excess baggage, give it to the poor, and work hard for the Kingdom of God.

(2) For the poor: don't worry, stop fighting, bear your suffering patiently for the love of God; you need very little to survive now, work hard for the Kingdom of God, very soon you will be with me in Paradise.

Prayer and mortifications - that is prayer of the senses - is the narrow road, the main weapon recommended by Our Lord and all those who followed him to Heaven; He said watch and pray always. This means holding on tightly to Jesus all the time with all our heart and minds, that is when He can protect us from all the evil and temptations in the world and take us to Heaven at the hour of our death. He said in the world we shall have troubles. I have overcome the world. (John 16:33).

Our Lady said by praying continuously we are pressing our head tightly against her chest for safety like a child on the lap of her mother. Without prayer we shall be overpowered by somebody, things, pleasure, vainglory, sensuality; one vice or the other, and at old age when there are no more activities we shall have a lot of problems with plenty of time with nothing to do - the beginning of Hell on Earth for those who do not love Jesus. Learning to pray is praying, not feeling; we have to force ourselves (Matt.11:12).

Since we are committing sins every day knowingly or unknowingly, the only way to appease God is by begging, so prayer is continuously begging God for mercy. When we start to lose our senses at old age, Prayer is a constant recollection.

Everybody on Earth is praying one way or the other, holding on tightly to the faith we profess; that is, what is dear to our hearts, for example money, vainglory, illusions, evil or Jesus for eternal life

WARNING! When the going gets tough, do everything within the teachings of the Church and do not let anybody deceive you. The true God said: "Deny yourself carry your cross everyday and follow me. I am with you always." Nobody on Earth can satisfy us. If we have to cry, do so; remember Jesus Himself wept. If we persevere we shall be getting tougher and tougher every day spiritually. By the age of fifty-five to sixty we should have succeeded in letting go of all childish and worldly rubbish, ready for home and able to say with St Paul: "It is not me that lives now but Christ lives in me"(Rom.8:10-11).

JESUS (EUCHARIST) MARY (ROSARIES)

THE CATHOLIC CHURCH (THE NEW ARK) ARE THE ANSWER

PRAYER TO ST MICHAEL

Holy Michael Archangel, defend us in the day of battle be our safeguard against the wickedness and snares of the devil. May God rebuke him we humbly pray; and do thou Prince of the Heavenly Hosts, by the power of God, thrust down to hell Satan and all other evil spirits who wander through the world for the ruin of souls.

AMEN

Letter From The Prison

Message of our Lady from Medjugorje, 25 May 1988

"Dear children!

"I am calling you to complete surrender to God. Pray, little children, that Satan does not sway you like branches in the wind. Be strong in God. I desire that through you the whole world may get to know the God of joy, neither be anxious nor worried. God will help you and show you the way. I want you to love all men with my love, both the good and the bad, only that way will love conquer the world. Little children, pray without ceasing so that Satan cannot take advantage of you. Pray so that you realise that you are mine, I bless you with the blessing of joy.

"Thank you for your response to my call."

JESUS (EUCHARIST) MARY (ROSARIES)
THE CATHOLIC CHURCH (THE NEW ARK)
ARE THE ANSWER

Letter From The Prison

Everyday Mental Activities of Three Categories of Men and Women

CATEGORY 1: very tough person. Ungodly, has no need of God, but has faith in him or herself; they think religion is for fools and cowards. (Psalm 52:1-9).

a. Always daydreaming and bent on fulfilling his or her dreams at all cost, full of schemes and worries for tomorrow that will never come.

b. Regrets for the past and blames something or somebody for it.

c. When not worrying, regretting, dreaming or busy, he or she is consoling him or herself with all sorts of devices mentally and physically.

d. Always doing everything possible to stay alive with the help of mortals like him or herself, with all sorts of medication and hoping for new inventions (Ps. 53).

They deserve pity and prayer because very soon he/she will get tired of running at old age and hand over the baton to somebody else to continue chasing the wind he or she never succeeded in catching (a vicious circle).

Sooner or later, he or she, his or her faith and toughness will all turn to dust. He will be forgotten because out of sight is out of mind (Psalm 37 and Psalm 73). Non-practising Catholics are in this category. Our Lady said, "Christians that do not pray are not Christians."

CATEGORY 2: cowards. Same as 1 above. Believes his/her God will make his/her selfish dreams come true, making his/her own will the will of God. They give up some visible vices, which are becoming too expensive for them anyway, to make a deal with this God and cover themselves with external virtues, and religious activities. People see through them; they are only deceiving themselves. God complained about them: "These people honour me with their lips but their heart is far from me" (Isa. 29:13-14)

They share the same characteristics as no. 1 with worse punishment because they are misleading others.

CATEGORY 3: fools. They renounce their own selfish dreams completely, but in all things seek only the will of God, his glory, salvation of souls and the world.

To the world they are fools; in reality they are the greatest and toughest human beings alive. They are the friends of God. They will never die, they will be happy for ever with God.

They cannot wait to leave this world and be with God, doing the minimum possible for their health and comfort.

Continuous conversion is going from 1-2-3 in a very few cases 1-3 with the help of Jesus and Mary through persistent and pondering prayer (rosary), self-denial and mortification; that is, interior struggles.

Characteristics of 1 and 2

a. We all want wealth, power, position, privileges, comfort and pleasure (human nature) seeking the praises of people.

b. We are always speaking of ourselves, even in our own praise, vaunting our good works past or present, our qualities or talents.

c. Gossiping and complaining. Crafty, always looking for somebody or people to use since they cannot be happy alone because, they have no God (Sirach 10:12-13).

d. Blame others, defend our own opinions obstinately, answer with bitterness; those who may contradict us because out of abundance of the heart the mouth speaks (Matt. 12:34).

Characteristics of 3

Always fighting his/her sinful nature and inclinations under all circumstances, working hard for his daily bread and doing good works for others, proclaiming the good news from day to day. Jesus, Mary, all the Angels and saints are with them always.

Their life on Earth will be lead by the Holy Spirit before going home. They can say with St Paul, "It is not me that lives now but Christ lives in me."

We are all women of Jerusalem; that is, pitying others instead of ourselves. For example, the unbelievers pity believers thinking that they are making life difficult for themselves whereas they deserve more pity because they are postponing the evil days till Hell or Purgatory.

Even now they are not happy; they have only sensuality with no peace of mind.

JESUS (EUCHARIST) MARY (ROSARIES) THE CATHOLIC CHURCH (THE NEW ARK) ARE THE ANSWER

Hail Holy Queen, Mother of Mercy, Hail our Life, our sweetness and our hope! To you do we cry, poor banished Children of Eve, to you do we send up our sights, mourning and weeping in this Valley of Tears. Turn then most gracious advocate Your eyes of mercy toward us, after this our exile show unto us the blessed fruit of thy womb, Jesus, O Clement O Loving O Sweet Virgin Mary.

Letter From The Prison

A Brief Meditation on the Rosary, Mysteries and Prayer

The Joyful Mysteries

1 Annunciation (Luke 1:26-38)
After four thousand years of waiting for a saviour, the news finally came to a teenager (thirteen to sixteen years of age), Mary, entrusted with such a responsibility, because God's ways are not our ways, his thoughts are not our thoughts. She never told anybody. This is the beginning of her interior agony, which ended at Christ's resurrection. She followed God from day to day through faith. This happened when she was praying quietly and listening to God. We should run away from noise and seek silence and solitude.

INTENTION - pray for the conversion of the whole world, that God should open our eyes and ears to see the miseries and nothingness of this world, and hear the voice of reason, so that we can stop chasing illusions and face reality God and Heaven.

"Our father", ten "Hail Mary", one "Glory be" and O "my Jesus, forgive us our sins, save us from the fires of Hell and lead all souls to Heaven, especially those who are in most need of your mercy. Amen."

Jesus have mercy on us, Virgin Mary help us.

May the souls of the faithful departed through the mercy of God rest in peace.

To be prayed after every decade of the rosaries.

2 Visitation (Luke 1:39-56)
Mary's four days' tedious journey to rejoice and help her cousin Elizabeth; and spirit of sacrifice the confirmation of angel

Letter From The Prison

Gabriel's message; John's response and sanctification by our lady in the womb. The magnificat - imagine the atmosphere of the household - Zechariah, a priest that had lost his voice, Elizabeth much older than Mary and pregnant, plus young Mary, work, prayer and contemplation (probably they are Essenes).

INTENTION - pray for the souls in Purgatory. If God should go by the rule, nobody will make Heaven, only by His mercies that people go to Purgatory; it is packed. These souls are in great torment; they are waiting for our prayers.

3 Nativity (Luke 2:1-20)
Mary and Joseph's obedience to Caesar Augustus's decree, an unbeliever in faraway Rome to fulfil prophesy. God is very much in control of the whole world; the hardship encountered despite carrying God in her womb, ended with animals. The first people to hear the news were shepherds, poorest of the poor, not the rich. The King of kings and Lord of lords came to his domain, nowhere for Him except the stable to undeceive the worldly spirit; upward mobility, the confirmation by the three wise men from the Far East. God is omnipotent. The envy of eighty-year-old Herod and God running away from Herod. The church has been under attack since then, and it will be so till the end of time. So is every individual Christian until death.

INTENTION - pray for the poor, oppressed and homeless the victims of the greedy and selfish world, winner takes all and remember your enemies too. (Maybe I am the one at fault; through prayer the Holy Spirit will enlighten me.) Most people live idle and sensual life - gossiping, dreaming, blaming the rich and Government for their misfortune.

4 Presentation (Luke 2:22-38)
Mary and Joseph lived a humble and lowly life, like any ordinary people. The priests and people never recognised Jesus, only Simon and Anna, both of whom are examples of piety - they were always in the temple praying. Another source of confirmation of who

Jesus is the Saviour.

And their obedience to the law of God.

INTENTION - pray for all parents looking after children, that God should help them lead their children and those under their care to God which demand a lot of effort sacrifice and prayer.

5 Finding of Child Jesus in the Temple (Luke 41-50)
Imagine the agony of Mary and Joseph for three days; doubts, guilt, regrets and so on. He was allowed freedom like other children, and that was why it happened. He was found in the temple not playing useless Roman games, but seeking God, His Father. Remember that they are human beings like us, apart from sins.

INTENTION - for all youths, that God should give especially those who are trying to live their faith in the midst of unbelievers, all the necessary courage and protection to persevere and through them they may come to know Christ, the Saviour of the world.

Sorrowful Mysteries

1 Agony in the Garden (Luke 22:39-46)
The King of kings, Lord of lords, who raised the dead, fed thousands from almost nothing, opened the eyes of the blind and performed an uncountable number of wonders, now afraid of suffering to the point of sweating blood. Unbelievable. Why? All the miracles are for our benefit to prove His divinity. God, now as man must atone for our sins. When the problem started, Jesus faced it squarely because He had been praying, but the disciples ran away, they had been sleeping. Learn to pray; learning to pray is praying.

INTENTION - pray for those in prison - one way or another we are all in prison - those sick at home, in the hospital, on the streets, mental homes, old people - we are becoming one every day - and those caring for them: prison staff and fellowships, doctors, nurses and hospital staff.

Letter From The Prison

2 Scourging at the Pillar (John 19:1-3)
The King of kings, Lord of lords, creator of Heaven and Earth, all things visible and invisible, being flogged by mare creatures, and He allowed it, for our sins. Whereas I deserve all my sufferings. Help me, Lord, to bear them patiently without bitterness or resentment.

INTENTION - pray for those seeking happiness of the senses and bodily pleasure to the detriment of their souls through vanity and the following industries: prostitution, pornography, smuggling, drugs, robbery, fraud and so on. One way or another I am involved in one or more of these industries. God give me the courage to stop, because I have no peace of mind, am never satisfied, always wanting more and more and more. Sooner or later I am going to get into trouble because nobody gets away with evil and come face to face with realities – Aids, jail, joblessness, homelessness, emptiness, injuries or death and miserable old age.

3 Crowning with Thorns (Matt: 27: 28- 29)
He willingly submitted to unlimited sufferings, ridicules and insults to expatiate our sins. No one can see his own faults; open my eyes, Lord, to see that I am as bad as those I ridicule, insult, criticise and so on. In other words, make me truly sorry for my sins and start loving instead; help me to learn from other people's mistakes.

INTENTION - pray for abandoned and aborted babies and those of us involved in this crime. This is the result of vanity and selfishness. What will people say? Greed and lack of self-control. Pray that God should open our eyes to see that these babies are flesh and blood like us, who want to live and enjoy life, and for those of us haunted by this crime, to be able to accept God's forgiveness and start a new life in Christ, and for those children abandoned by their parents to the mercy of technology.

4 Carrying of the Cross (John 19:17)
All these sufferings are for our sins. After two thousand years look around; everywhere is sin galore; we are all waiting for the Government, the Church, or super powers and so on to do

something. No! Every individual must renounce his/her sins and cling to Jesus for salvation; nobody can do it for you or me. We came alone into the world from God; alone we shall go back to him; not as an African or rich or poor; alone.

INTENTION - pray for all priests, the religious, seminarians, novitiates: they are at the forefront of these spiritual battles against evil. Pray that God protect them from all temptations from within their parishes and in the world and help them to be faithful to their vows, to fill them with abundance of the Holy Spirit so that they can save souls from this very dark and unbelieving world under the mask of religion, virtues and civilisation, modern paganism. Pray also to call people to this vocation; we need more priests and religious workers. Also pray for the conversion of youths.

5 Crucifixion (Luke 23:46-43)

The King of kings, Lord of lords allowed himself to be killed, again for our benefit, because the ultimate end product of everybody we can think of is dust (death). His main mission on Earth was to destroy death forever. Mary at the foot of the Cross, a pillar of faith; only God knows how much she suffered spiritually from annunciation; remember she was like us in every way, but without sin; she followed God day by day with trust.

Her part in the process of redemption is next to God since the Holy Spirit and Jesus are all the same God. Thank God for a good mother, mediatrix of all graces.

INTENTION - I commit my own spirit into the hands of God now, because I don't know the minute or hour when the Lord shall come. Pray for those in their last agony; prepared, that is, with a priest, viaticum and well-wishers; with prayers of divine mercy and rosaries, wishing him or her a very safe journey home, with a very sure hope of seeing him or her very soon at the feet of Christ and our Lady saying: "God be with you till we meet again." And for those not prepared, that God should have mercy on their souls.

Letter From The Prison

Glorious Mysteries

1 Resurrection (Mark 16:6)
The core of the Christian message: that after death we shall rise again with Christ. Without this message there is no Christianity and life has no meaning. Trapped in ourselves because of selfishness, greed and sensuality, the main characteristic of every human being, we cannot see the nothingness of this world and the miseries of our neighbours, thereby aiming for a better life promised to us by Jesus.

INTENTION - pray for all Christians that God should give us all the courage necessary to practise and proclaim our faith under any circumstances we may find ourselves, thereby saving the world for God. All we have to say is – You can believe whatever you like; but as for me, Jesus is my Lord and Saviour and Mary is my Mother, they will raise me up when I die and take me to heaven – no fighting.

2 Ascension (Mark 16:19)
Proved beyond reasonable doubt that there is life after death; that Jesus is God and has opened the gate of Heaven for anyone who wants it. By His examples, teachings and commandments, He showed us the way to follow Him. We are not robots. God gave every individual free will; hence it is up to you and I to make the decision, to follow Jesus to Heaven or stay behind in Hell; it is our choice - not even God will force us.

INTENTION - pray for unbelievers and enemies of the Church all over the world that God should open their eyes because they are fighting a losing battle. One with God is a majority and change their hearts. They did not create themselves, but are biting the hand that feeds them. They are definitely not happy; only sensuality; that is, pleasure of the body and senses with no peace of mind: self- deception. They are pretending to be happy because the only source of happiness is God, through Jesus Christ our Lord.

3 Descent of the Holy Spirit (Acts 2:4)

God is not in a hurry, only men, women and the world; running at increasing speed every day to nowhere with too much noise. It took four thousand years to fulfil His promise; the Israelites lived in Egypt for four hundred and thirty years before deliverance; the child Jesus stayed in the womb of Mary for the normal nine months; He grew up like a normal child; stayed at home for thirty years before commencing His ministry; after His ascension He asked His disciples to wait in Jerusalem. In real life we are always waiting for something; finally at old age, death. This God is still the same today, yesterday and forever. Let us learn patience. Without the Holy Spirit nobody can live a good Christian life and understand spiritual things; without faith in Jesus and His Church we cannot have the Holy Spirit. The Apostles were like you and me; carnal and sensual, they found it hard to understand Jesus and His spiritual teachings for three years, until they were filled with the Holy Spirit.

INTENTION - pray for abundant pouring of the Holy Spirit upon the Holy Father, the Pope, the clergy and the whole Church, that they should continue to guard and protect the eternal truth taught by the son of God, despite all attacks from within and without.

4 Assumption of Our Blessed Lady (Rev., Apoc. 12:1)

The reward of her suffering and the first fruit of the new life. Let us hold tightly to our rosaries, praying continually for all her intentions; that is, for others not ourselves; as mediatrix of all graces she knows what we need; she will take care of us. She is still suffering in a way, because many of her children are refusing to respond to her call for conversion, still choosing death instead of life. She loves us all equally, both good and bad.

INTENTION - pray for peace in the world; lack of peace is due to selfishness and greed; that God should enlighten our hearts to know that the only thing worth fighting for is Heaven and the weapon is love.

Letter From The Prison

5 Coronation (Judith 15:9-11)
What eyes have never seen, what ears have never heard of, is what God has prepared for us in Heaven. Jesus said, "In my Father's house there are many mansions; I am going there to prepare a place for you; where I am you will be there also." Considering death it is very obvious that this world is not our home.

INTENTION - thank God for all the graces He has bestowed upon us through the intercession of Our Lady, queen of peace.

The Mysteries of Light

1) Christ's Baptism in the Jordan (Mark 1:10), His hidden and ordinary life for thirty years and His humility. We pray that God should protect us from pride – an inordinate Love of our own glory, our deadliest enemy. This is encouraged by the secular world for money's sake.

2) Christ's self-revelation at the Marriage of Cana (John 2:11), He proved His divinity by changing water into wine through the intercession of His Mother, Mary, and <u>by his present</u> approved normal social and married life. We pray for married couples, broken homes and single parents.

3) Christ's proclamation of the Kingdom of God with His call to conversion (Mark 1:15). After two thousand years there are still plenty of sins around, mainly because of too many false teachers promising miracles and comfort to people in the name of Jesus instead of repentance and penance. We pray that God should vanquish heresy in the world.

4) Christ's transfiguration (Matt. 17:2). He showed the disciples a glimpse of the future glory in Heaven. If there is no Heaven life is meaningless. We pray that God should give us the strength and courage to carry our crosses till the last day of our life on Earth.

5) Christ's institution of the Eucharist (Luke 22:19) - the heart of the Gospel. He made Himself available for anybody who wants Him, anywhere and any place all over the world as a means of unifying His followers. We pray that God should increase our love of Jesus in the Eucharist, which can touch every individual's heart, because nobody on Earth has power over anybody's heart.

JESUS (EUCHARIST) MARY (ROSARIES)
THE CATHOLIC CHURCH (THE NEW ARK)
ARE THE ANSWER

BECAUSE WE ARE ALL SINNERS AND WE ARE GOING TO DIE SOME DAY, THAT IS WHY THE ROSARY IS THE BEST OF ALL PRAYERS.

PRAY FOR US SINNERS NOW AND AT THE HOUR OF OUR DEATH

AMEN